T0132041

A Special Christmas

Written by Anina Leigh

WestBow Press books may be ordered through booksellers or by contacting:

WestBow Press
A Division of Thomas Nelson & Zondervan
1663 Liberty Drive
Bloomington, IN 47403
www.westbowpress.com
844-714-3454

ISBN: 978-1-6642-2501-5 (sc)
ISBN: 978-1-6642-2502-2 (e)

Library of Congress Control Number: 2021903655

Print information available on the last page.

WestBow Press rev. date: 10/12/2021

Matthew 1:23 - Behold, a virgin shall be with child, and shall bring forth a Son, and they shall call his name Emmanuel, which being interpreted is, God with us.

Alexander
Lane
1512

The kettle was beginning to whistle. Tea cups were prepared to receive the hot liquid. What perfect makings for hearty warm refreshments on this cold icy evening.

Steam had formed around the windows drawing one to review the images outside. This picture held scenes of fresh fallen snow silently glazing the tree branches; leaving reflections of a beautiful Christmas. It left one to ponder the weather conditions of when our Savior was born. Yet, a sigh was all one could hear as they viewed the heaps of icy snow leading to the impossibility of going any where.

Psalm 36:6 You Lord serve both people and animals

The Alexander family had endured many struggles but there was never an excuse to not help people. Like the time the Jeremiah family barn caught fire, burning it to the ground. They were devastated. Not thinking twice, the Alexanders packed a meal for all the families and headed to the farm up the road.

As everyone was discussing the damage, a large lumber truck approached. The driver honked and waved and they could see it was Lee from the sawmill in town. As he stepped down from the truck, he stated that the delivery was a gift from their neighbors, the Alexander family. The crowd cheered and began unloading the lumber. Soon the barn would stand again.

Matthew 2:11 O come let us adore him

Celebrating Jesus' Birthday was the perfect time to come together and share all the many blessings The Lord had bestowed upon everyone during their trials and tribulations. Yes, this would indeed be a very Special Christmas.

Family

The sight and aroma of a huge Evergreen Tree adorned with trimmings seemed the only way thankfulness could be shared. But How? It would take a miracle. A Big Miracle!

The snow touched every area of that home place. It left few options of getting a tree in there, much less in time for Christmas. Let's see...hummmm...well, the plow wouldn't work... It was broke. Someone would have to go into town and get materials to make repairs...so that was not Happening! The tractor? it wouldn't get very far and kept conking out. That was not Happening! Saddle one of the horses? Chop the tree and pull it? ...Too hard on the horse in this zero weather. It just wasn't possible! They could walk but by the time they found a tree they would be worn out and no way to haul it back. So, that was not Happening either. They were totally deadlocked.

Actually, there was only one thing to do.. THEY COULD PRAY! Prayer changes things they say---that was it... the only option. So the family found their way around the table, joining hands,and bowing their heads. Someone began to pray. Oh, it was a simple prayer. It went something like this...Dear Lord, if there is any way we can celebrate your birthday with a real live Evergreen Tree standing big and tall in our living room, will you please have it delivered here because there is no way for us to go out there and bring one inside. We thank you Lord. Amen

All the family returned to the joys of Christmas. Setting the table. Baking pies. Wrapping gifts. Pure merriment had hit the house by storm. Singing broke out...Over the hills we go laughing all the way... It was such fun singing and imagining the tree all lit up with colored lights, ornaments, tinsel, candy canes and presents---

Suddenly, in the far distance, seemed a sound of a motor of some sort. Goodness who or what can it be? The sound came nearer to the house. It was sputtering and then revving up. Yes, there was something definitely headed their way. Everyone ran to the windows, watching... waiting and holding their breath.

Merry Christmas
Florida

All at once, all could see the shine of small headlights coming in to meet at the roads end. Who could it be... heading down the home driveway ever so slowly? The lights would flicker, but kept steady on the snowy trail, puttering along. After what seemed like hours, all could clearly see a Big Red Truck! Hanging from it were long green branches. A small truck followed close behind it, carrying many colored lights. Tears of joy filled the eyes of the entire family. Could this be the answer to the prayer?

Merry Christmas!
Merry Christmas!

Both trucks pulled right to the edge of the porch steps. "Good evening everyone! Merry Christmas!", shouted Lee, from the truck full of lights. Then the sawmill owner, Doug, explained that the Evergreen tree was being delivered as a Thank You for all the lumber that had been purchased". That large order had allowed his sawmill to continue operations through the Christmas season.

Psalm 72:19 Blessed be his glorious name forever;
may the whole earth be filled with his glory!

The Miracle Had Occurred! A huge Evergreen Tree with many colorful lights to celebrate the birth of Jesus. This was the most Beautiful Tree they would forever live to tell.

What a Special Christmas indeed.

Isaiah 49:23 Burst in to song all you mountains, you forests, you trees.

Oh Christmas Tree, Oh Christmas
Tree How faithful are thy branches.

Repeat

Oh Christmas Tree, Oh Christmas Tree
Green not alone in summertime
but in the winters frost and rime:

Oh Christmas Tree, Oh Christmas Tree
How faithful are thy branches.

Finally, the tree was placed in the center of the room, decorated with all the trimmings as the presents lay beneath it.

It was time for Doug and Lee to go, so everyone headed outside.

Goodbye and thank you again for the magnificent Christmas Tree.

Happy Holidays!

Merry Christmas!!

In the stillness of the evening were the sounds of a train... chugga chugga, wooo hoo!, whoo hooo!.... The family found themselves waving and shouting "Merry Christmas everyone!".... as they watched the train wind its way through mountains and valleys, it reminded them that although life has rises and falls, Just Trust the Lord and Enjoy the Ride.

Prayer:

Dear Lord,

Thank You for Your Special Gift of Christmas, and may we always share Your Light to guide others to You...our Wonderful Savior. In Jesus Name, Amen.

Traditional Christmas Decorations and What They Represent:

1. Christmas Tree: The triangular shape of the Fir Tree is used to explain The Father, Son and Holy Spirit.

2. Star: Symbolizes the Star of Bethlehem, leading the Wise Men to where Baby Jesus lay.

3. Angel: The term "angel" literally means "messenger", just as an angel appeared to Mary, with the message of the birth of Jesus.

4. Lights on the tree: Resembles the lights from the night sky.

5. Tinsel: Represents little sparks from the fire made by Joseph to keep Mary and Jesus warm during their stay at the stable.

6. The colors on the Christmas Tree:
   Red: Is for Jesus' Blood that was shed to redeem us.

   Silver and Gold: Are for the rich blessings that Jesus has given us.

   Green: Is for the plants and trees God provided as food for us.

7. Candy Cane: Reminds us of the Shepherd's staff of Jesus, leading his flock and the shepherds being the first witnesses of his birth.

8. Wreath: Represents the unceasing love of The Father. It shows how God's mercy is renewed every morning and how His love has no beginning or end.

9. Gifts under the Christmas Tree: Gifts hung on the tree and under the tree, remind us of how we receive the greatest gift on earth, which is "Eternal Life" through the blood of Jesus Christ.

10. Ornaments: Became a tradition that brought family and their friends together to decorate the tree and celebrate the birth of Jesus.

11. Bells: The significance of the Christmas Bells is that they ring out to guide the lost sheep back to the shepherd.

12. Christmas Bows: Indicates that we should all be tied together with bands of good will forever.

13. Christmas Candle: The candle light represents the welcoming of the Christ Child and how He is The Light of the World. It also guides us through darkness.

14. Trains Around the Tree: Symbolizes the coming and going of packages and shipments that increased during the Christmas season.

    Also, running a train around the Christmas Tree brings back memories of simpler times.

    And...

    Family times of returning home, as in the 1940's when the railroad helped hundreds and thousands of G.I.'s to...

"Be Home For Christmas".

About the Author

Anina Leigh learned that the desires of her heart became real with just a simple prayer.

She wanted to write a Christmas Story for Christmas Eve. The family gatherings were always filled with joy and excitement. This year she would surprise them with a special reminder of God's goodness and how he genuinely answered prayers.

Anina Leigh could have never imagined the doors of opportunities that followed. They would be only ones The Lord himself could open. Her desire to write, suddenly blossomed into plans far beyond her expectations.

As you go with her in this journey of the Christmas Tree, be encouraged that you, too, can pray a simple prayer and watch God's plans designed for you be unlocked and delivered.

Printed in the United States
by Baker & Taylor Publisher Services